Anonymous

Ball Electric Light Company

Manufacturers of the Ball Electric Light System for all purposes of

illumination

Anonymous

Ball Electric Light Company
Manufacturers of the Ball Electric Light System for all purposes of illumination

ISBN/EAN: 9783337270230

Printed in Europe, USA, Canada, Australia, Japan

Cover: Foto ©Andreas Hilbeck / pixelio.de

More available books at **www.hansebooks.com**

Ball Electric Light Co.

404 West 27th St.

NEW YORK

MANUFACTURERS OF THE

BALL ELECTRIC LIGHT SYSTEM

FOR

ALL PURPOSES OF ILLUMINATION.

OFFICES: 404 WEST 27TH STREET.

FACTORY: 281 TO 289 NINTH AVE. AND 400 TO 416 WEST 27TH ST.

NEW YORK CITY.

WE install plants on 30 days' approval for all bona-fide and responsible would-be purchasers; when, if we fail to satisfactorily perform our contract stipulations, we will remove the apparatus at our sole cost.

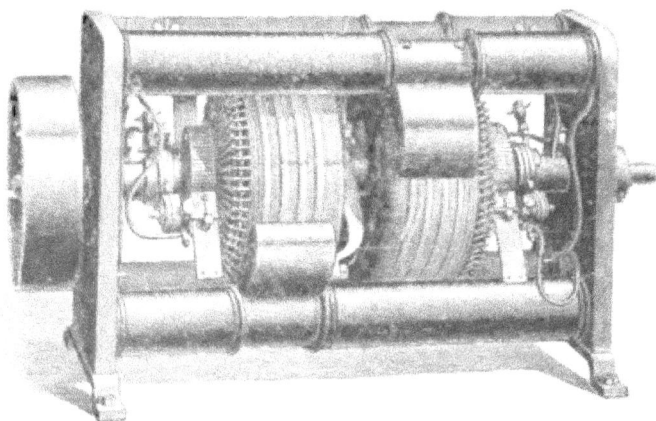

THE ELECTRIC LIGHT

Is not in its infancy, as is often claimed by people who have no practical knowledge of the subject; it is now well developed and understood, and is evidently the artificial light which will be chiefly used for municipal and business purposes in the future. The great advantage of the electric light is in the volume of light afforded, and that buildings are illuminated by its use to an extent impracticable through the use of gas or oil. The *cost* of electric lighting is usually no greater than gas—in many cases is far less ; and when the volume, purity, safety and healthfulness of the light are taken into account, it is in all cases the most desirable.

4

THE BALL SYSTEM OF ELECTRIC LIGHTING.

THE Ball Dynamo has now been in general use throughout the United States, Canada, Great Britain, South and Central America, and the Republic of Mexico for the last ten years, and its many advantages are so well-known, that we do not propose to go extensively into its electrical and mechanical points of superiority.

We wish, however, to impress the public with the fact that *our double armature dynamos have the same advantage over single armature dynamos, that the double cylinder or compound steam engine has over single cylinder engines.* This advantage, is of course, most noticeable in power saved, but it also makes a showing in the steadiness of the Ball Arc Lamps, to which the Ball Dynamo supplies a perfectly steady and constant current, and the mechanism of the lamps is such as to feed the carbons positively and regularly, and thus constantly maintain an Arc of defined length, between the carbon points, thus doing away with the hissing and flickering which are so common in all other systems and especially noticeable in them when carbons are feeding.

The durability of the Ball Dynamo is principally due to the double armature feature on account of small amount of wire necessary to produce the required force and therefore less heating from resistance of said wire. The splendid workmanship and quality of material used in the construction of our dynamos are universally acknowledged.

We have built our present improved dynamo for ten years past, which fact gives us ground for making such broad claims regarding our system.

THE BALL

Sub-Divided Arc Light System.

More Economical and Superior to Incandescent Lights for
Street and Commercial Lights in Cities, Towns
and Villages, Car and Machine Shops, Depots, Mills
and Manufactories.

MANUFACTURED SOLELY BY

BALL ELECTRIC LIGHT COMPANY,

NEW YORK CITY.

FACTORY : CORNER 27TH STREET AND 9TH AVENUE.

OFFICES : 404 WEST 27TH STREET.

PHENOMENAL SUCCESS

HAS ATTENDED THE INTRODUCTION OF THE

BALL ECONOMY

ARC LIGHT SYSTEM.

Long Arc.—800 actual candle power. 4 ampere current. E. M. F. 49 volts
Over 3 lights to the horse power.

☞ The Arc is not sub-divided horizontally (by using low voltage which would produce a poor light), but quantity of current passing is divided, and higher electro-motive force used, thus maintaining a long Arc.

We call your special attention to **our** sub-divided, 4 Ampere, 800 candle **power** arc light.

We confidently believe that we can to-day offer you the most economical, noiseless and steady arc light known.

We guarantee to produce these lights on less than one-third of a horse-power each, and the economy in the introduction of this dynamo as compared with incandescent lighting can readily be seen. In producing a light of this power and cheapness we believe that we fully overcome the objections heretofore raised to the use of arc light in machine shops, stores and factories, as the lesser cost per light and the economy in running will enable the purchaser, by installing a slightly larger number of the 800 c. p. arcs, to thoroughly distribute the light, thus overcoming the shadows from the more powerful arc lights, and thoroughly light his premises at much less expense than by any incandescent system. The sub-divided 800 c. p. arc will also, in our opinion, supersede the 1,200 and 2,000 c. p. lights for town and village lighting where shade trees have made economical lighting by lights of large candle power an impossibility.

The novelty and merit of this system of arc lighting has become so thoroughly demonstrated that it has been adopted by a large majority of purchasers after investigating apparatus of larger candle power of our own and other Company's manufacture.

We have sold the 4 ampere system for the past six years, so purchasers can be assured that it is no experiment ; but at the same time *no other Company has been able to produce this class of light,* nor is it possible to with any other machine than the BALL DOUBLE ARMATURE DYNAMO.

We continue to make as before, our 6, 8 and 10 Ampere Dynamos and Lamps with the same attention to mechanical and electrical detail, **good** work and superiority of finish, that has in the past secured for them a national reputation.

7

THE BALL DYNAMO.

THE important factor in all systems of electric lighting is the DYNAMO, or *Current Generating Machine.* These machines are all based upon the same general principle; all generate currents in the same manner, and with the single exception of the BALL DYNAMO, all machines bear a striking resemblance to

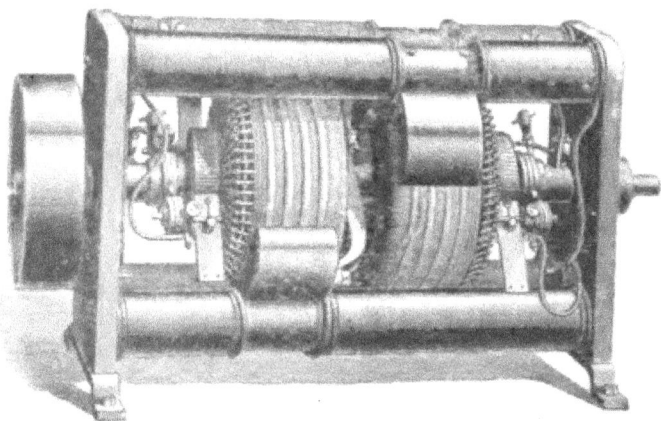

BALL DYNAMO.

each other in the essential elements of their construction, the current being generated in *one* armature. which is rotated within the influence of both the poles of a powerful electro-magnet.

The BALL DYNAMO has *two* armatures, each being rotated within the influence of the separate poles of an electro-magnet.

8

This construction **has been** proved **to** possess great merit, and the BALL DYNAMO is constructed with *less material,* has *less internal resistance,* has *greater efficiency,* generates *less heat,* and to give *equal* results requires *less **power*** than any other dynamo in the world.

The greatest difficulty with which electricians **have** to contend in the construction and operation of electric current generators, is the electrical heat developed by **the** current within the coils and armatures **of** the machines, which chars the material **with** which the wires are covered, and destroys the insulation. **The** BALL DYNAMO *does not heat.*

The speed of the machine can be increased **to** furnish current for 50 per cent. more lamps than **its** nominal capacity, without danger of charring **the** insulation of the wires, so free from heat is the BALL DYNAMO, while the speed of single armature Dynamos cannot be materially increased without great **danger of** immediate destruction. The single armature Dynamos **in** the market are rated **at the** full capacity to which they can be run, while the **BALL** DYNAMOS, **as rated,** have **a very** large margin for safety against injurious heat.

THE BALL DYNAMO

Has the Following Advantages over all Others:

It produces a more constant and uniform current, and far more *clear, steady* and *noiseless light*. It requires no cooling, regulating or safety devices whatever.

It will *outlast* any other Dynamo, as the normal heat generated within it is much less, and more readily radiated

It does not require to be run at an exact speed, and any power of ordinary uniformity will produce good results.

It is the only *Dynamo that will not overheat when subjected to the variable speed of engines used in mills, factories, etc. Overspeeding does not affect it*

It does not require the attendance of an expert; any intelligent man can quickly be taught to operate it with success.

It has made the longest continuous runs of any Dynamo yet constructed without heating.

It has been in practical operation for ten years, and has been subjected to more severe tests than any other machine in the market.

It has extraordinary efficiency, and leaves but little, if any, room for improvement in electrical generation by induction.

Its mechanical construction is of the best. The shaft is hammered steel, ground to standard size, the bearings gun metal, the frame forged iron, surface ground and finished bright. The workmanship will bear the closest inspection. The wear of commutators and consumption of brush copper is very slight.

It requires but *three-fourths* of one horse-power to produce each full arc light of 2,000 candle-power.

It requires *but one-third of one horse-power* to produce *each full arc light of 800 candle-power.*

It requires but *two-thirds of the power required by other Dynamos* to produce an equal amount of light.

It is equivalent to two Dynamos of any other make, for the reason that if one armature is disabled by accident, the other armature will maintain nearly three fourths of the full number of lights.

It will give more perfect results with less skilled attendance than any other Dynamo.

It can operate Arc or Incandescent Lights separately, or both in combination, in one circuit, or in two separate circuits, at the same time.

BALL COMMUTATOR.

CONSTRUCTION PATENTED.

The Ball Commutator is composed of a number of pure copper sections, separated and insulated one from the other by thick strips of mica. The pins or arms connecting segments to armature are thoroughly insulated, the interstices being filled with the best insulating webbing or filling. The advantages of this mode of building a Commutator are too apparent to need comment.

BALL ARMATURE.

BALL ARMATURE (PATENTED).

The Ball Armature consists of an endless iron ring entirely surrounded and covered by an endless coil of insulated copper wire —the best high-tension armature made. It is impossible, with this armature, to be troubled by its striking through or burning to core, as the core is electrically connected with nothing, and protected for all time, by its continuous and solid surrounding of insulated copper wire, from having its insulation affected by dust, oil or moisture.

THE BALL SYSTEM OF ELECTRIC LIGHTING.

We offer the BALL System on its merits, and invite thorough investigation as to its superiority in all matters of detail. We claim for it durability and simplicity, and the maximum of economy in cost, operation and maintenance, **as compared** with any other system. We claim much, but not more **than we are** prepared to prove and perform.

LIST OF ARC DYNAMOS

Designation of Machine.	No. Lights 2,000 c.p. 10 amp. X	No. Lights 1,600 c.p. 8 amp. Y	No. Lights 1,000 c.p. 6 amp. Z	No. Lights 800 c.p. 4 amp.	Horse-Power at Pulley of Dynamo.	Width of Single Belt in in.	Belt Speed Required	Weight of Dynamo.	Length.	Width	Height.
C	8	....	....	....	6.5	1¼		530	3'5"	1'2"	1'9"
C	...	10	....	....	6.3	1¼		530	"	"	"
C	....	....	....	25	8.0	2		530	"	"	"
E	16	...	....	....	12.0	2½		780	3'10"	1'4"	1'10"
E	....	20	....	....	12.5	2½		780	"	"	"
E	....	...	26	....	13.0	2½		780	"	"	"
F	20	...	....	....	15.0	3		990	4'2"	1'7"	1'11"
F	....	25	...	....	15.6	3	5,000 FEET PER MINUTE	990	"	"	"
F	....	...	32	....	15.0	3		990	"	"	"
F	....	....	....	50	16.0	3		990	"	"	"
G	28	...	....	....	21.0	4		1,360	4'5"	1'8"	2'00"
G	...	35	....	....	21.0	4		1,360	"	"	"
G	....	....	45	....	21.0	4		1,360	"	"	"
G	....	....	....	70	21.0	4½		1,360	"	"	"
H	40	....	....	....	29.7	6		1,750	5'3"	1'11"	2'5"
H	....	50	....	....	30.0	6		1,750	"	"	"
H	....	....	64	....	29.5	6		1,750	"	"	"
I	52	..	....	....	38.0	8		2,290	5'8"	2'1"	2'8"
I	....	65	....	....	38.6	8		2,290	"	"	"
I	....	....	83	....	38.0	8		2,290	"	"	"
J	64	..	....	....	46.5	10		2,770	6'0"	2'2"	2'9"
J	...	80	....	....	47.1	10		2,770	"	"	"
J	....	....	100	....	45.5	12		3,200	6'2"	"	2'10"
K	75	....	....	....	52.5	12		3,200	"	"	"

We offer to the public the BEST SYSTEM OF ELECTRIC LIGHTING in the world—the most economical in operation, the most easily cared for, the most durable, the cheapest in cost—and invite inquiries and correspondence from parties interested.

SINGLE ARMATURE ARC DYNAMOS

	No. Lights 2,000 c.p. 10 amp.	No. Lights 1,600 c.p. 8 amp.
L	4	5
M	8	10
N	10	12

These are our only Dynamos with single Armature—are the least expensive, but of excellent efficiency, and suitable for small requirements.

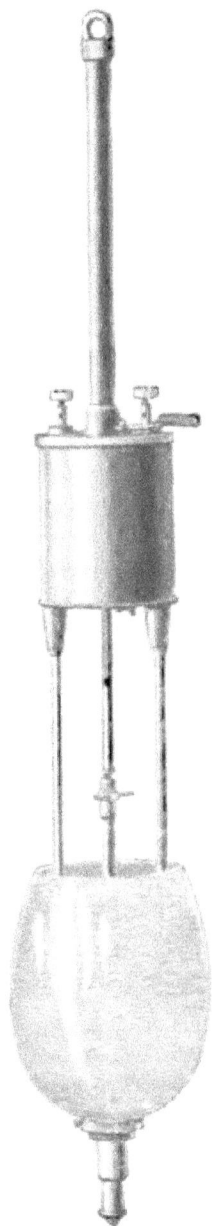

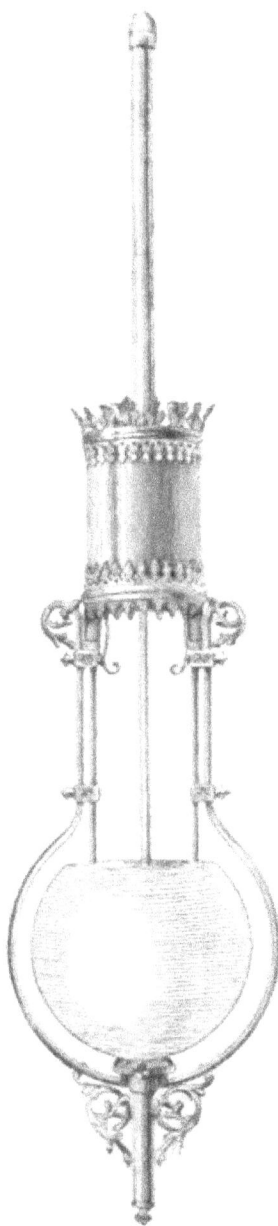

BALL SINGLE AND ORNAMENTAL LAMPS.

THE BALL ARC LAMPS

Are of neat appearance and substantial construction. There are no springs, friction clutches
or glycerine dash-pots in them to lose adjust-
ment, but every movement is positive and
mechanical. They do not wear or get out of
order, and will run for years without repairs and
with but slight attention. Their operation is
unaffected by vibrations caused by storms, or
jarring from machinery or other causes, and will
be found reliable at all times. They do not
"burn out," neither do they require constant
cleaning and watching, as do those of other
systems. The light given is white, powerful,
steady and *noiseless.*

Our lamps can be adjusted to burn on any
system or circuit, either arc or incandescent.

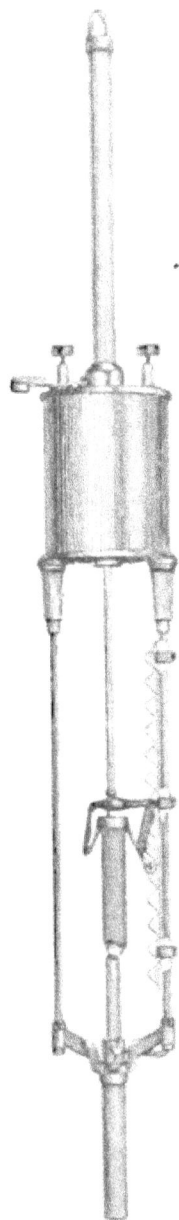

BALL RECIPROCATING CARBON ALL-NIGHT LAMP.

The Ball Reciprocating Carbon All-Night Lamp.

We have lately introduced a new, all night, single carbon lamp, which has all the advantages of the double, triple and disk carbon lamps, but is free from their many disadvantages as to unreliability, complicated mechanism and constant repairs.

This lamp is materially cheaper in first cost, and is far more economical to maintain than either of the above, requiring less time to trim and less care and attention to keep in proper working order.

As will be seen by the accompanying illustration, an attachment (covered by patents) is placed on our regular lamps by the use of which they can be made to burn any length of time required, without changing carbons.

This result is attained by reciprocating or swinging the top or positive flat carbon across the bottom or stationary round carbon; the former being made, of course, with a greater cross section than the latter.

Thus, as the upper carbon wastes away and is fed to the arc, it is periodically moved across the arc so as to consume one portion after another.

The reciprocating, or oscillating movement is accomplished by the use of a device (as will be seen from cut) which moves in a downward direction, at the same time feeding the upper carbon and giving it a "to-and-fro" or swinging movement over the bottom stationary round carbon.

By this arrangement the point or crater of the upper carbon is kept in line with the point of the negative or bottom carbon, thereby producing a quiet, non-shifting or traveling arc.

The light given by this lamp is powerful, steady, free from all shadows, hissing and flickering, common to all other lamps.

By placing the Ball Reciprocating Carbon Lamps on the market, we believe we have supplied a long-felt want for a reliable means of all night lighting. Wherever these lamps have been used, their many points of superiority have become so thoroughly demonstrated that, they have at once taken precedence over all others.

The Ball Long Distance Series Incandescent System.

We take pleasure in calling the attention of our customers and friends to our New Improved Series System of Incandescent Lighting.

We have recently perfected a **New** Automatic Dynamo, possessing one of the **simplest,** most sensitive and reliable regulators known, and having adopted a well-known Series Lamp **with** combination socket and cut-out, we are fully prepared **to** furnish a complete system, unequalled by any in the market.

Of over 10,000 lamps equipped with **these sockets** and cut-outs, we have yet to learn **of an** instance where the latter have failed **to** perform **their** work in closing the circuit, in event **of** a lamp burning out, **or** in **case** of a lamp having been taken from its socket.

It is not necessary however, to detail **the merits of** these lamps and sockets here; suffice it **to** say, **that** the series lamp, as far as brilliancy and **economy are** concerned, is acknowledged to be far superior to all others.

These lamps are of low resistance, durable and efficient, remaining bright throughout their entire service.

In the Series System, as signified by its name, the lamps are **run** in series on a single circuit of variable electro-motive force, but on a small constant current of 4 **or** 6 amperes,

Number 8 wire is sufficiently large to use in connection with any installation of the Ball Series System, *no matter how many lamps are in circuit, nor the distance they are from the generator or station.*

Copper conductors are the most expensive part of a large incandescent plant, and the saving in conductors or copper by using the series instead of the parallel or converter systems, would in a fair sized installation alone pay the total cost of a series plant.

We give below a table showing the amount of copper conductors required by the various systems, together with the cost of same. based on a plant of 500 lights capacity, where the centre of distribution is 1,000 feet from the generator, and the farthest light 4,000 feet, figuring wire, for convenience, at 15 cents per pound.

System.	Current Employed	Voltage	Designation of Wire	Pounds of Wire Required	Total Cost @ 15c. per lb.
Parallel	Direct	110	Thirty No. 0000	107,920	16,188
Three Wire	Direct	220	Nine No. 0000	31,920	4,788
* Transformer	Alternating	1,000	No. 2	1,180	177
Series	Direct	Varies according to number of circuits used.	No. 8	780	117

* Exclusive of Converters.

It will thus clearly be seen that the saving of the Series System over the parallel in a plant of this description would be $16,071; over the three wire $4,671; and over the transformer (not taking in consideration the many pounds of wire used in converters, a very important item,) $60.

The Series System must not be confused with the dangerous alternating or converter system, nor with the parallel or three wire system—with their tons of copper conductors and their high amperage—a great danger arising therefrom on account of fire.

We simply use a No. 8 wire, carrying a small 4 or 6 ampere current, as the case may be, and a limited voltage.

With our Double Armature Dynamo the output may be divided into two independent circuits, if desired ; thus, it is apparent that by the use of these two circuits the total electro-motive force of the apparatus can be halved.

If the Series System is installed in a good manner, with the best insulated wire, and kept free from " grounds," the danger to human life is reduced to the minimum.

Having given a brief description of our New Improved System, we will sum up some of its important advantages over all other incandescent systems as follows :

Lowest in first cost.

Most economical, both as to power and running expenses.

Best regulation.

Long life of lamps.

Most brilliant lamps.

Greater reliability, simplicity, and efficiency.

Different degrees of illumination possible, and the perfect control of the light, as well as the small cost at which it may be profitably furnished.

Flexibility of distribution.

Wide areas and thinly settled districts that may be advantageously served.

Possessing these merits, the Ball Series System is able to overcome many of the difficulties which have heretofore retarded a full development of the practical sub-division of the electric light.

We claim our series system to be the cheapest method of electric lighting ever devised, and challenge competition in the production of light per horse-power at any distance, with less outlay for station equipment and copper conductors than required by either the parallel or transformer systems.

Plants of our system may be located where power and labor are the cheapest, even though they be miles from the centre of distribution, without employing any large mains, transformers or converters, regardless of the number of lamps in circuit, or the candle power of same.

Arc Lamps on Incandescent Circuits.

Arc lamps, in connection with the incandescents, can be successfully operated on the Ball Series System without affecting the brilliancy or the steadiness of the latter.

We earnestly invite a thorough examination and trial of our new system, which we feel confident will meet all the requirement of parties desiring a first-class system of incandescent lighting.

N. B.—Motors may be operated, and storage batteries charged by the Ball Series Incandescent System.

BALL IMPROVED SERIES SYSTEM

GIVES COMPLETE SATISFACTION

For Long Distance Incandescent Lighting.

LAMPS ARE PERFECTLY STEADY, BRILLIANT AND OF LONG LIFE.

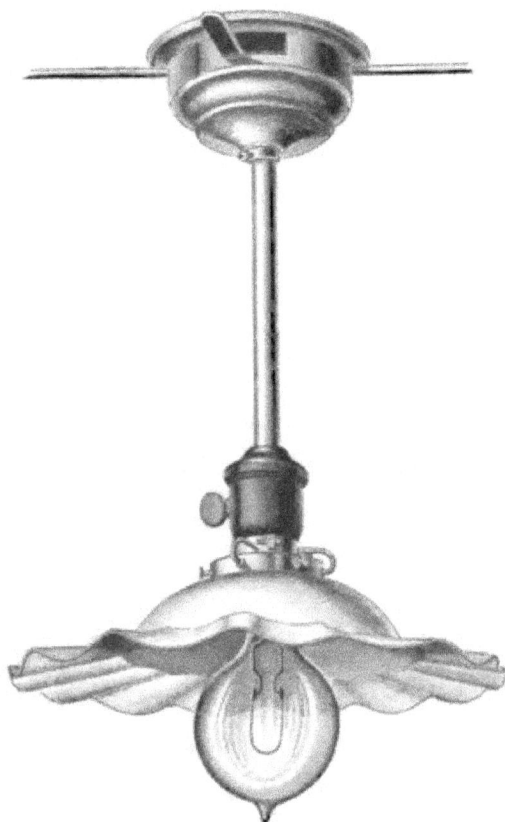

OVER 10,000 OF THESE LAMPS IN USE ON BALL CIRCUITS,

Throughout the United States, Canada, Mexico, South and Central America.

23

Our Long Distance Incandescent Dynamo

Has the same advantages over other Incandescent Dynamos that our Arc has over other Arc Dynamos.

It has, like the Arc, two armatures, is self regulating, and will carry from one up to its rated capacity without attention, and therefore we offer with it none of the mechanical devices and attachments necessary with the Dynamos of other systems.

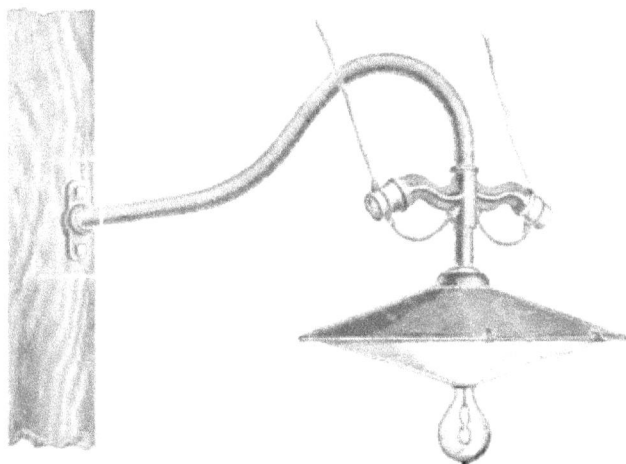

STREET FIXTURE, AS IN USE.

List of long distance Incandescent Dynamos, based on lamps of 3.2 watts, efficiency per candle power.

Designation of Machine.	Capacity in 16 c.p. Lights.	Capacity in 25 c.p. Lights.	Horse-Power at Pulley of Dynamo.	Width of Single Belt in inches.	Belt Speed Required.	Weight of Dynamo.	Size in Inches.			Revolutions per minute.
							Length.	Width.	Height.	
O	100	63	8.2	2		550	3' 3"	1' 2"	1' 9"	1600
P	150	93	13.1	2½		790	3' 10"	1' 4"	1' 10"	1420
Q	200	126	16.4	3		1000	4' 2"	1' 7"	1' 11"	1350
R	275	173	21.2	4½	5 000 FEET PER MIN.	1380	4' 5"	1' 8"	2' 00	1225
S	350	220	30.0	6		1800	5' 3"	1' 11"	2' 5"	1150
T	460	287	38.5	8		2320	5' 8"	2' 1"	2' 8"	1080
U	560	350	47.5	10		3050	6' 2"	2' 2"	2' 9"	1010
V	670	420	53.	12		3350	6' 3"	2' 2"	2' 9"	980

Lamps, Sockets, Street Fixtures, etc., on the most favorable terms.

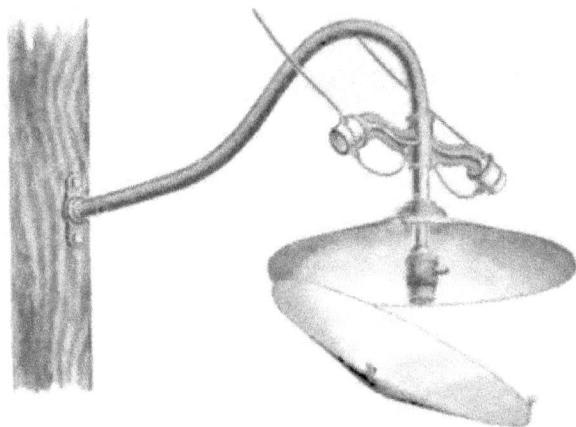

We ask intending purchasers to write for quotations before purchasing elsewhere.

BALL ELECTRIC LIGHT CO.

GUARANTEES.

We Guarantee our 4 ampere or 800 c. p. Dynamo to give the most perfect results for MANUFACTURING ESTABLISHMENTS and for Street Lighting. Power required less than 1-3 of a horse-power per light.

We Guarantee our 6 ampere or 1,200 c. p. Dynamo does not require over 1-2 h. p. per light.

We Guarantee our 8 ampere or 1,600 c. p. Dynamo does not require over 65-100 h. p. per light.

We Guarantee our 10 ampere or 2,000 c.p. Dynamo does not require over 8-10 h. p. per light.

We Guarantee our Dynamo will give much greater efficiency than any other for given metal. **power** and kind of work.

26

Don't forget that the test of time has proved the armatures of most systems to be short lived, and that when they burn out the manufacturers generally explain that it must have been caused by lightning or over-speeding. These causes never harm the Ball armatures.

FACTS.

Our Dynamo is about one-half the weight of Dynamos of other systems carrying the same number of lights.

Our Dynamo requires no foundation, but can be placed without bolting down on the floor of any building.

Our Dynamo will outlast the Dynamos of any other system.

Our Dynamo is perfect in regulation, requires the least amount of attention and repairs of any in the world.

Our Lamp is purely mechanical, and does not depend upon springs and dash-pots for its proper working.

Our Lamp does not burn out, neither does it require constant cleaning.

Our Lamp is not affected by thunder-storms, nor extinguished by blasting or like causes.

NO OTHER SYSTEM POSSESSES THESE ADVANTAGES.

Any ordinary mechanic can install and successfully operate the " Ball System " without the aid of an expert or electrician.

CORRESPONDENCE SOLICITED.

ESTIMATES FURNISHED FOR ARC OR INCANDESCENT PLANTS.

Read the Following:

Remember that we are prepared to give the best results for the least money.

Remember that we can operate any number of Incandescent Lights in connection with the arcs *on the same* circuit, regardless of its length.

Remember that both our Arc and Incandescent Dynamos are absolutely perfect in regulation.

Remember that our (Double Armature) Dynamos are virtually equivalent to two of other systems, for the reason that in case of accident to one armature the other will maintain from $\frac{1}{2}$ to $\frac{2}{3}$ the full rated capacity of lights.

Remember that we guarantee any City or Town *One Hundred and Fifty Arc Lights* from a *Fifty Horse Power-Engine.*

ASK ANY OF OUR COMPETITORS IF

THEY WILL DO IT?

Remember that if you use Coal the wise thing to do is to burn as little as possible.

Remember that our Dynamos excel in efficiency, execution, and economy of cost and maintenance, any known system.

Remember that we make a *100 Light Dynamo*, 1,200 c. p., and guarantee it shall maintain the 100 lights *Over Fifty Miles of Wire,* thereby making a large saving in the cost of operation, if water power can be obtained anywhere within a radius of Twenty-five miles from the centre of distribution.

Remember that no other company can furnish the above apparatus.

BALL ELECTRIC LIGHT COMPANY,

404 WEST 27TH STREET,   NEW YORK CITY.

TESTIMONIALS.

HARTFORD **ELECTRIC LIGHT** CO.

HARTFORD, CT., January 6th, 1892

BALL ELECTRIC LIGHT Co.,

New York.

Gentlemen—Yours of January 2d at hand. In regard to your system will say we are running five of your fifty light, and one one hundred light, Ball dynamos. *They have been running about five years*, with the exception of the 100 light machine which **we** started last May. They are all running **very** nicely and satisfactorily. We are running about 275 **of** the Ball single lamps, which are also working very satisfactorily, with *very little expense for repairs*. Think we shall have another 100 light machine in the near future.

Yours respectfully,

HARTFORD ELECTRIC LIGHT CO.

PROVIDENCE, R. I., January 21st, 1892

BALL ELECTRIC LIGHT Co.,

New York.

Gentlemen—We **have** been running one 35 light and **two 50** light, Ball dynamos since June, last, with entire satis-**faction**. Our lights, 122 in all, are distributed on three circuits, one of which runs all day, the others when we want them. *A test showed that less than 45/100 horse-power per light is consumed in the production. The lamps are nominal 1,200 c. p., but they appear as brilliant as those formerly used, which were nominal 2,000 c. p.* The dynamos require but little attention. We believe the Ball is the *most economical* **dynamo** that has been brought **to** our attention.

Yours truly,

CALLENDER, McAUSLAN & TROUP CO.

GULF COAST AND ICE MANUFACTURING CO.

BAY ST. Louis, Miss., Feb. 2, 1892.

BALL ELECTRIC LIGHT CO.,

New York

Gentlemen—Replying to your **letter of the** 29th inst., would respectfully say that we **are using one** of your 70 light, 4 ampere dynamos, with 25 800 **candle power arc** lamps and 150 series incandescents, **which have proven** entirely satisfactory.

We think it has **no** *equal as far* **as** *quality* **and** *steadiness of lights are concerned,* and we consider **we are making a** *material saving in the expense of running* **same on account** *of dynamos taking less power than those* **of any other make.** We would recommend your system **to** any parties who **are** interested in electric lighting, and cheerfully extend **the** privilege of **using** this letter in connection therewith if **you** so desire.

Yours, etc.,

PAUL CONRAD, Prest.

ABINGDON WATER WORKS CO.,

ABINGDON, VA., January 14th, 1892.

BALL ELECTRIC LIGHT CO.,

New York.

Gentlemen—Your favor of **the** 12th inst. at hand, and noted. In reply will state that about two years ago we built our plant and installed your system of arc service. We **have** therefore been using your system for two years, and we **have** been more than pleased with it, and have never regretted our **choice.** We are operating 22 1,600 candle-power lamps. **Ten** of these are **on our** streets, and the remaining twelve **on** commercial lights. Two of the twelve are in the Methodist Church here, the largest con-

31

THE NATIONAL STARCH MANUFACTURING CO.

GLEN COVE, L. I., April 30th, 1892.

BALL ELECTRIC LIGHT CO.,

New York.

Gentlemen—In reply to yours of the 25th inst., would **say** that the Arc machine you furnished us about *six years ago* is now, and always have been, *working to our entire satisfaction.* It is of 25 light capacity, and we have in use from **18 to 20** lights.

Yours truly,

NATIONAL STARCH MFG. CO.

WAMSUTTA MILLS.

NEW BEDFORD, MASS., January 22, 1892.

BALL ELECTRIC LIGHT CO.,

New York.

Gentlemen—Your letter of January 12th received. Should have been answered before but writer has been very busy, and has not had time. Would say that we have **two** 70 light machines and one 25 light, making a total of one hundred and sixty-five (165) lights. These have been running **since** October, 1889. The light burns steadily, and gives **satisfaction** to both employer and employees.

Yours respectfully,

WM. J. KENT, AGT.

J. G. BRILL COMPANY.

CAR BUILDERS,

62d Street and Woodlawn Avenue,

PHILADELPHIA, PA., January 14th, 1892.

THE BALL ELECTRIC LIGHT CO.,

404 West 27th St., N. Y. City.

Gentlemen—We take pleasure in sending a testimonial to you of the electric light plant which you have lately

*Don't be deceived by ready-tongued agents, often found **with** systems of electric lighting **not** possessing intrinsic **merit** and genuine worth.*

---

furnished us for our works. The dynamo **is the largest, we** believe, in use in Philadelphia, being of **1,200 candle power** each. The greatest number of **lamps that we have been** using from this dynamo up to the **present** time is ninety-**two, and** they give an admirable **and** steady light. *The **dynamo is** operated **with ease by** the Armington-Syms 50 horsepower engine,* running 275 revolutions per minute, at eighty pounds steam pressure. You are **at** liberty to bring any of your friends here to see the machine in operation at **any** time, **and we** will show it **with pleasure.**

Very truly yours,

G. MARTIN BRILL,

President and General Manager.

UNION SQUARE PANORAMA CO.

NEW YORK, February 3d, 1892.

BALL ELECTRIC LIGHT CO.,

New York.

Gentlemen—For lighting our picture building **and for** advertising purposes we have employed for the **past** *five years* a " Ball Plant " for **two** dynamos and forty arc lights. *The service has been continuous, **three** hundred and sixty-five nights in the year.* It has been trustworthy, complete and satisfactory. The *cost for repairs and replacement has been very small,* and our electrician takes pleasure **in** speaking **in** the highest **terms of the efficiency and** reliability of the plant.

Yours truly,

UNION SQUARE PANORAMA CO.

OYSTER BAY ELECTRIC LIGHT & POWER CO.

OYSTER BAY, L. I., March 10th, 1892.

BALL ELECTRIC LIGHT CO.,

New York.

Gentlemen—Yours of the 8th inst. at hand, and in reply to same would state that I have **built, set and** handled

We guarantee our 6 ampere or 1200 c. p. dynamos not to require over ½ h. p. per light.

machinery **for over 18 years; but when** I first started the Ball dynamo **I was** surprised that the machine required so little attention, and when we were up to full capacity and had **to** exchange the same for a larger one, I was afraid that there could not be another machine built that would give as **good** satisfaction **But, to** my surprise, **we** have it. Some **of the** good qualities may be due to the fact that we use water power, which my experience leads me to believe is the steadiest and most reliable power in the world. Our lamps **give** universal satisfaction, and it is of every day occurrence **to have people comment on** them **and** say *they are a fine light and the* steadiest they *ever saw.* From the time of **starting to** the time of shutting **down,** *our* machines require *no more* attention than a grinding-stone

D. D. SMITH.
Vice-Pres. and Supt.

ELLENVILLE, N. Y., March 20th, 1892.
BALL ELECTRIC LIGHT CO.,
New York.

Gentlemen—We have had the 50 light machine purchased of you in constant use since we started up the first of last November. We use water power, and *don't believe* **any one** *makes a nicer arc light than we do.* We couldn't ask **for a** better machine.

Very truly yours,

ELLENVILLE ELECTRIC CO.,
E. D. RUSSELL, Treas.

THE EAST SHORE TERMINAL COMPANY.

CHARLESTON, S. C., January 20th, **1892**.
BALL ELECTRIC LIGHT CO.,
New York.

Gentlemen—The East Shore Terminal Co. has been using two of your 25 arc light dynamos for the past seven months. Forty-one arc lights and fifteen to twenty 32 candle power incandescent lights have been in constant use,

and run from 15 to 16 hours out of the 24, and it is with
pleasure that I say they have given first-class satisfaction in
every respect.

Yours respectfully,

CHAS. W. TOWSLEY, Supt.

DICKSON MANUFACTURING COMPANY.

SCRANTON, PA., January 14th, 1892.

BALL ELECTRIC LIGHT CO.,

New York.

Gentlemen—Yours of the 12th inst. is received. We
are running 67 lights with three of your machines (one
30 and two 20 light). These are, as you are aware, machines
that had been used by the Scranton Electric Light & Heat
Co. *about 6 years* before we took them—about *2 years ago.*
They still give us very good satisfaction.

Yours truly,

WM. HERKINS, Treas.

READING, PA., January 13th, 1892.

BALL ELECTRIC LIGHT CO.,

New York.

Gentlemen—For the use of Rolling Mills and Manufacturing interests of that kind, we think the Ball machine
is one to serve that purpose best. We have had the system
in use for the past *6 or 8 years*, running 7 arc lights in the
Mill and some 8 or 10 incandescent lights in the office.
The power is derived from a general line of shafting running
the shears, fans, pumps, etc. The machine sustains the
varied speed usual to such conditions without any noticeable injury. The *repairs are extremely moderate*, and the
benefits in increased light as compared with coal oil or gas
are immensely in favor of electric light at a cost very much
less.

WM. McILVAIN & SONS.

37

MINERVA CAR WORKS,

MINERVA, Ohio, February 17th, 1892.

BALL ELECTRIC LIGHT Co.,
New York.

Gentlemen—We have your inquiry of recent date, and are pleased to say that we have had one of your 25 light dynamos of 2,000 candle power, each, in constant use since July, 1888, and to this date *not one dollar has been expended for repairs* to the dynamo. Two or three lamps being accidentally broken has been our only expense for repairs. The machinery never refused to work satisfactorily, and has always been operated by an ordinary engineer.

Yours truly,

PENNOCK BROS.

BESSEMER ELECTRIC COMPANY.

BESSEMER, ALA., January 23d, 1892.

BALL ELECTRIC LIGHT Co.,
New York.

Gentlemen—We have been using one of your sixty light machine and lamps for over one year, and are very much pleased with them. *For economy of power and efficiency in lights, as* **well** *as durability, they cannot be excelled.* They have cost us nothing for repairs, and we cheerfully recommend **your** system to all in need of arc light.

Yours respectfully,

BESSEMER ELECTRIC CO.

WEYBOSSET MILLS.

PROVIDENCE, R. I., January 13th, 1892.

BALL ELECTRIC LIGHT Co.,
New York.

Gentlemen—In reply to your favor of **the** 12th, I would say that we have **70** arc lights furnished by your establishment. They **have** been in operation about *five years*, and their duty has **been** satisfactory.

Yours, etc.,

WEYBOSSET MILLS.

PHOENIX WOOLEN COMPANY.

EAST GREENWICH, R. I., January 21st, 1892.

BALL ELECTRIC LIGHT CO.,

New York.

Gentlemen—We have in use two of your 50 light machines which have run about four years to our entire satisfaction. Thirty-eight lights have been used for street lighting, and the others for Mill and were we to increase our plant should do so by adding more of your machines.

Yours truly,

PHOENIX ELECTRIC LIGHT & **COAL CO.,**
JOSEPH DEWS, President.

PORTSMOUTH GAS & ELECTRIC CO.

PORTSMOUTH, O., January 16th, 1892.

BALL ELECTRIC LIGHT CO.,

New York.

Gentlemen—Your plant consisting of one 70 light and one 50 light dynamos has been in operation very nearly two years running from 70 to 105 lights (commercial arcs.) My predecessor spoke of the working of the plant during the period of its installation until he left in July, 1891, in the very highest terms, and during the six months of my administration here, I find no word except of commendation necessary.

Yours truly,

PORTSMOUTH GAS & ELECTRIC **CO.,**
T. A. BATES, Supt.

CLYDE BLEACHERY AND PRINT WORKS.

RIVERPOINT, R. I., February 13th, 1892.

BALL ELECTRIC LIGHT CO.,

New York.

Gentlemen—Yours of the 26th at hand, and would say we put down our first Ball dynamo over seven years ago,

39

Our dynamos will not overheat when subjected to the variable speed of engines in factories, etc.

which **was** displaced by a larger one, and then another large **one** added, both giving a capacity of 80 arc lights, 1200 c. p. Of these we **are** using at present 65 lamps. The dynamos are driven 1400 revolutions per minute ; the 45 lamp machine with a 4 inch belt, and the 35 lamp machine with a 3 inch belt (both double). The *expense for* **repairs** *of the dynamos is trifling* in amount. It would be **difficult** to persuade us that there is a better arc light **system than** the Ball for either outside or inside lighting, **and we have** both **in use.**

Yours truly,

S. H. GREENE & SONS.

THE SPENCER GAS COMPANY.

SPENCER, MASS., January 5th, 1892.

BALL ELECTRIC LIGHT **Co.,**

New York.

Gentlemen—We have used 70 arc electric lights, 1200 **c. p.,** Ball system, to light the streets of Spencer the past **four** *years, and don't want anything different.*

SPENCER GAS CO.,
L. HILL, President.

ERIE & WESTERN TRANSIT COMPANY.

CHICAGO, ILL., **July** 1st, 1891.

BALL ELECTRIC LIGHT CO.,

New York.

Gentlemen—This is **to** certify that we have used the Ball eight hundred candle power system for the past three years, using 7/16 carbons, with an average run of nine hours, without recarboning. It answers our purpose first-class, and *we want no other.* We can't speak in too high praise for it, and those who are connected with it.

Yours respectfully,

ERIE & WESTERN **TRANSIT CO.**

ICE FACTORY, ELEC. LIGHT & COLD STORAGE.

LAKE ST. CHARLES, LA., February 6th, 1892.

BALL ELECTRIC LIGHT CO.,

New York.

Gentlemen—Your favors of January 7th and 21st duly to hand, and we beg to apologise for our tardy acknowledgment of same. We are thoroughly well pleased with our entire system. The dynamos are wonderful power **transmitting** machines, taking into **consideration** their **very** small size. They run very light and very **steady,** and **owing to** the double armature feature, they run perfectly **cool.** The two dynamos bought of you have been **in** constant **use for** nine consecutive months, and have **never** caused **us the** slightest uneasiness. We have never dropped the current after once starting up during the entire period. We have had *no repairs or breaks.* In fact, *we have **not spent one** cent on them* during the entire time, and they **seem** in **as** perfect condition as when they were first put in operation. The two dynamos referred to were sold us **for 70** arc light machines of 800 candle power per arc lamp.

We are now operating seventy **arc** lamps, one hundred and forty 16 c. p. incandescent lamps, and sixty-four 25 c. p. incandescents. These lamps **are** strung on 12½ miles No. 8 wire, and these two machines will stand **a** few more lights without detracting from their full effectiveness. The arc lights though rated at only 800 c. p., each, are from expert testimony, really from 1200 to 1600 **c.** p. each. *The light from them is very steady and bright.* The incandescents also give a good, steady, bright light.

The prominent features about your system is that both **arc** *and incandescent are operated from the same dynamo and from the same wire.* The above mentioned plant yields us a revenue of $530 monthly. The cost of operation monthly is $238. This includes electrician, lineman, trimmer, fireman, fuel, etc., rating our fuel at $2.25 per cord **for** pitch pine wood. The cost of operation to our company, in connection with our other enterprises, does not amount to half of the above estimate which is made independent of our other enterprises, or what it would actually cost us **to** operate the plant independently.

Wishing you the success you so **well** deserve, **we are,**

Yours truly,

J. A. LANDRY & CO.

41

Our dynamos require the least amount of attention and repair of any in the world.

PARTIAL LIST OF BALL PLANTS.

Our dynamos are not over one-half the weight of dynamos of other systems carrying the same number of lights.

A

Aguirre, J. & Sons	Mexico, Mex.
Almonte Electric Light Co. (increased)	Almonte, Canada
Almolonda Elec. de Quezaltenango (inc)	Quezaltenango, Guat.
American Optical Co.	Southbridge, Mass.
American Net and Twine Works	Boston, Mass.
Aylmer Electric Light Co. (increased)	Aylmer, Canada
Ashuelot Valley Elec. Light Heat & Power Co.	Winchester, N. H.
Abbott Machine Co.	Chicago, Ill.
Abbott & Sons, J. L.	Mason City, Ill.
Abingdon Water Works Co.	Abingdon, Va.
Arnprior Electric Light Co.	Arnprior, Ont.
Arthur Electric Light Co.	Arthur, Ont.
Agricultural Exhibition Society	Victoria, B. C.
Abell, John	Toronto, Ont.

B

Bell Light and Power Co.	Montgomery, Ala.
Beaver Head Hydraulic Mining Co.	Idaho
Belleville Gas Co. (increased)	Belleville, Ont.
Benton, F. E. (incandescent)	Fairchild, Wis.
Bennett, Nelson (2 plants)	Cascade Tunnel, W. T.
Dent, W. M. & Co. (increased)	Chicago, Ill.
Berglund, R. J.	Minneapolis, Minn.
Berlin Gas Co. (increased)	Berlin, Ont.
Boggs & Buhl	Allegheny City, Pa.
Boies Car Wheel Works	Scranton, Pa.
Bowmanville Electric Light Co. (increased)	Bowmanville, Ont.
Brantford Electric Light Co. (increased)	Brantford, Ont.
Brill, J. G. & Co. (increased)	Philadelphia, Pa.
Brockville Gas Co.	Brockville, Ont.
Bush Mfg. Co.	Fitchburg, Mass.
Bessemer Electric Co.	Bessemer, Ala.
Brady Bros.	Inman, N. Y.
Blanco y Trigueros	San Salvador, C. A.
Brooklyn & Rockaway Beach R. R.	Canarsie, N. Y.
British American Starch Co.	Brantford, Ont.
Bracebridge Electric Light Co.	Braceford, Ont.
Brussels Electric Light Co.	Brussels, Ont.
Barrie Electric Light Co.	Barrie, Ont.

C

Campbell & Hitt   Frankford, Pa.
Campbell & Dick   Pittsburgh, Pa.
Carillie, I. (Increased)   Maracaibo, S. A.
Carleton Place Electric Light Co   Carleton Place, Ont.
Centennial Brewery   Philadelphia, Pa.
Central Pacific Milling and Manufacturing Co., Redwood City, Cal.
Chandler Electric Light Co   Halifax, N. S.
Chatham Gas Co.   Chatham, Ont.
Chester Pipe and Tube Co   Chester, Pa.
Chicago Arc Light and Power Co   Chicago, Ill.
Chrome Steel Works   Brooklyn, N. Y.
Cincinnati Ice Mfg. and **Cold** Storage Co   Cincinnati, Ohio.
Clark's Cove Guano Co.   **New** Bedford, Mass.
Clark Insurance Electric Wire Co   Bristol, Pa.
Clarksburg Electric Light Co   Clarksburg, W **Va.**
Clarry Wool and Manufacturing Co. (increased) Markham, Ont.
Cleghorn Mills   Fitchburg, Mass.
Clyde Bleaching and **Print** Works **(increased)** Riverpoint, R. I.
Combination Iron and **Steel** Co   Chester, Pa.
Cottage City Gas Co   **Martha's** Vineyard, Mass.
Crowe Iron Works   Guelph, Ont.
Cyclorama Co   Boston, Mass.
Cyclorama Co   New York City.
Cyclorama Co   Philadelphia, Pa.
Chicago Oyster House   Chicago, Ill.
Consolidated Electric Light **Co**   Birmingham, Ala.
Cincinnati Electric Light Co   Cincinnati, Ohio.
Catasauqua Mfg. Co.   Catasauqua, Pa.
Callender, McAustom & Troup **Co**   Providence, R. I.
Consolidated Electric Light and **Power Co** Kansas City, Kansas.
Cannington Electric Light Co   Cannington, Ont.
Corporation of Picton   Picton, Ont.
Colborne Electric Light **Co**   Colborne, Ont.
Chesley Electric Light Co   Chesley, Ont.
Central Bridge Works   Peterborough, Ont.
Corporation of North Toronto   N. Toronto, Ont.
Corporation of Toronto Junction   Toronto Junction, Ont.
Corporation of City of Victoria   Victoria, B. C

D

Dominion Barb Wire Co. **(increased)**   Montreal, Que.
Dominion Bridge Co   Montreal, Que.
Dominion Bridge Co   Toronto, Ont.
Doty Engine Co. (increased)   Toronto, Ont.
Douglas, Wm. A. & Co   Leadville, Col.
Dunlap, Rob't & Co. (Incandescent)   Brooklyn, N. Y.
Dunnell Manufacturing Co   Pawtucket, R. I.
Dickson Mfg. Co   Scranton, Pa.
Durham Electric Light Co   Durham, Ont.
Dresden Electric Light **Co**   Dresden, Ont.

E

Erie Basin Dry Docks . . . . Brooklyn, N. Y.
Erie & Western Transit Co . . . . . . Chicago, Ill.
East Shore Terminal Co . . . . . . Charleston, S. C.
El Paso Electric Light and Power **Co** . . . . El Paso, Texas.
Ellenville Electric Light and Power **Co** . . . . Ellenville, N. Y.
Enterprise Coal and Supply Co., Lim . . . . New Orleans, La.
Espinosa, Miguel (increased) . . . . . . Merida, Yucatan.
Electric Construction Co . . . . . . Greenwich, N. Y.
Exeter Electric Light Co . . . . Exeter, Ont.

F

Fechemmer Bros. **& Co** . . . . . . **Cincinnati, Ohio.**
Fredericton Gas **Co** . . . . **Fredericton, N. B.**
Freeman Lon . . . . **Chicago, Ill.**
Forest Electric **Light Co** . . . . **Forest, Ont.**

G

Galaxy Mills . . . . Minneapolis, Minn.
Gananoque Electric Light Co **(increased)** . . Gananoque, Ont.
Glen Cove Manufacturing Co . . . . . . Glen Cove, N. Y.
Globe Iron Works . . . . Cleveland, Ohio.
Godfrey Pocket Co . . . . Plymouth, Mass.
Goldie & McCulloch (increased) . . . . . . Galt, Ont.
Granite Mills . . . . Pascoag, R. I.
Grimsby Park Co (increased) . . . . . . Grimsby, Ont.
Groff, C. M. . . . . Reading, Pa.
Grommes & Ulrich . . . . Chicago, Ill.
Guelph Gas Co (increased) . . . . . . Guelph, Ont.
Galvanotype Engraving Co . . . . . . New York City.
Gilbert, B. F. . . . . Tacoma Park, Washington, D. C.
Gulf Coast Ice Mfg. Co . . . . . . Bay St. Louis, Miss.
Groton Bridge Works Co . . . . . . Groton, N. Y.
Grand Haven Electric Light and Power Co . Grand Haven, Mich.
Gignon & Co., A . . . . Quebec, Que.

H

Hamilton Tool and Bridge Co . . . . . Hamilton, Ont.
Hanlan's Point Ferry Co. (increased) . . . . . Toronto, Ont.
Hartford Electric Light Co. (increased) . . . . Hartford, Conn.
Heat, Light and Power Co . . . . . . Muncie, Ind.
Hinckley, F. E. . . . . . . Wellston, Ohio.
Hotel San Rafael . . . . . . San Rafael, Cal.
Holmes Co., The P. C. . . . . . . Gardiner, Me.
Hagersville Electric Light Co . . . . Hagersville, Ont.

I

Ingersoll-Sergeant Drill Co . . . New York City.
Iron Bay Mfg. Co. (2 plants) . . . Marquette, Mich.
Iron Silver Mining Co. (2 plants) . . . Leadville, Col.
Island Park—Toronto City Corporation . . . Toronto, Ont.

J

Jersey City Electric Light Co **(increased)** . . Jersey City, N. J.
Jordan, Marsh & Co . . . . Boston, Mass.

K

Kingston & Pembroke Railway Co . . . . .   Kingston, **Ont.**
Kirksville Electric Light, Heat and Power Co . . . Kirksville, **Mo.**
Keefe, M. H . . . . Bush-Ivanhoe Tunnel, Busk, **Col.**
Keeseville Electric Light and Power Co   Keeseville, **N. Y.**
Kincardine Electric Light Co . .   Kincardine, **Ont.**

L

Lake Hopatcong Hotel Co . . . . **Lake Hopatcong, N. J.**
Lansdale Electric Light Co . . . . **Lansdale, Pa.**
Lion Brewery . . . . **Philadelphia, Pa.**
London Electric Light Co. (increased) . . . . **London, Ont.**
Long Branch Park Co . . . . **near Toronto, Ont.**
Liddell & Co., Forbes . . . . **Montgomery, Ala.**
Landry & Co., J. A . . . . **Lake Charles, La.**
Loraine Mfg. Co . . . . **Pawtucket, R. I.**
Lovejoy, Frederick (incandescent) . . . . **Yacht "Neiera," N. Y.**
Lea & Sons Co., Wm . . . . **Wilmington, Del.**
Lindsay Electric Light Co . . . . **Lindsay, Ont.**
Lucknow Electric Light Co . . . . **Lucknow, Ont.**
Leamington Electric Light Co . . . . Leamington, **Ont.**
Lakefield Electric Light Co . . . . Lakefield, **Ont.**

M

Macullar, Parker & Co . . . . Boston, **Mass.**
Manton Mills . . . .   Manton, **R. I.**
Massey Mfg. Co   . . . .   Toronto, **Ont.**
Manz & Co . . . . Chicago, **Ill.**
McAlpine, The Geo. **W. & Co. (increased)** . . . Cincinnati, Ohio.
McCauley, Buckwalter **& Co** . . . . Westchester, Pa.
McDonald & Bros . . . . La Crosse, Wis.
McDougall, A. & Son, **Distillers** . . . . . . Halifax, N. S.
McHose, Isaac & Sons . . . . Norristown, Pa.
McIlvain, Wm. & Sons . . . . Reading, Pa.
Moss Park Skating Rink Co . . . . Toronto, Ont.
Mt. Forest Electric Light Co. **(increased)** . . Mt. Forest, **Ont.**
Munson, C. A., Steam Dredge . . . . . . Belleville, **Ont.**
Moss Engraving Co, ... New York **City.**
Murray & Datz . . . . Rockaway Beach, **N. Y.**
Metropolitan Lumber **Co** . . . . Metropolitan, **Mich.**
Murray & Kemp . . . . Delhi, **N. Y.**
Mt. Morris Ill'g Co . . . . Mt. Morris, N. Y.
Melchers, Successors . . . . Mazatlan, Mexico.
Montreal Rolling Mills . . . . Montreal, Que.
Milton Electric Light Co . . . . Milton, Ont.
Midland Electric Light Co . . . . Midland, Ont.
Mimico Asylum . . . . Mimico, Ont.

N

Napanee Paper Co   Napanee, Ont.
National Worsted Mills (increased) . . .   Olneyville, R. I.
Newmarket Electric Light Co. (increased) .   Newmarket, Ont.
Newport Light Co. (increased)   Newport, Ky.
New Haven Copper Co   Seymour, Conn.

BALL ELECTRIC LIGHT COMPANY,

REPRESENTED BY

H. M. FRENCH,
63 Equitable Building, Boston, **Mass.**

E. O. PARTRIDGE,
356 "The Rookery," Chicago, **Ill.**

ENTERPRISE CONSTRUCTING & SUP. CO., L<small>D.</small>,
167 Gravier St., New Orleans, **La.**

NOVELTY ELECTRIC COMPANY,
50-54 North 4th St., Philadelphia, Pa.

PIONEER ELECTRICAL COMPANY,
Aberdeen, S. D.

GEORGE W. FINCH,
Escanaba, Mich.

MARTINDALE & LAKE,
Chattanooga, **Tenn.**

BALL ELECTRIC LIGHT COMPANY, L<small>D.</small>,
Toronto, Ontario.

I. L. PICKLE,
Abingdon, Virginia.

A. J. MYERS,
Oakland, Cal.

SKILTON & SON,
31 Broadway, New York.
Agents Central and South America, Cuba and West Indies.

48

WE offer to the public the BEST SYSTEM OF ELECTRIC LIGHTING in the world—the most economical in operation, the most easily cared for, the most durable, the cheapest in cost —and invite inquiries and correspondence from parties interested.